The Freechild Project Youth-Driven Programming Guide

Adam Fletcher

THE FREECHILD PROJECT YOUTH-DRIVEN PROGRAMMING GUIDE
Copyright © 2015 Adam Fletcher

Published by CommonAction.
Olympia, Washington 98507-6185

commonaction.org

In honor and memory of my mentors as a youth, including Idu, Jamie, Steve, Margaret, David, John, Bill, and Helen.

You set the course for this work to begin.

Contents

ADAM FLETCHER

Section 1.

About Youth-Driven Programming

Youth-Driven Programming is any deliberate activity youth lead for purposes that benefit themselves and others.

For more than 15 years, The Freechild Project has been working to connect young people and social change in communities around the world. In our continued work to transform the roles of young people throughout society, we have developed our model of Youth-Driven Programming. It is our focus for organizational development.

As long as community work specifically focused on youth has existed, adults have been designing, facilitating, and evaluating it. However, over the last twenty-some years, many nonprofits, schools, and government agencies have discovered the reward of fostering youth voice throughout their operations affecting youth. Years of research and best practice have led to the development of a model to foster the growth of this activity, and it is called Youth-Driven Programming.

Youth-Driven Programming is a guiding philosophy and practice for organizations that want to transform the roles of young people in their communities. Youth-Driven Programming goes beyond simply listening to Youth Voice and toward integrating youth as partners throughout organizations and communities.

Section 2.

What's the Difference?

Traditional Youth Programs	Youth-Driven Programs
✘ Adult designed	✓ Youth designed
✘ Adult facilitated	✓ Youth facilitated
✘ Adult evaluated	✓ Youth evaluated
✘ Youth compliance is key	✓ Adults as support
✘ Youth are forced to attend	✓ Youth attend on their own

Youth-Driven Programming is different from traditional youth programming in many ways. The differences become apparent in the premises or assumptions behind the program to the activities youth do to the funding the program receives and the ways it is evaluated. There are distinct differences.

The primary ways traditional youth program models treat youth is obvious from their focus. Most traditional youth programs either see youth as receptacles, recipients, informants, and promoters.

As **receptacles**, activities and ideas treat youth as empty containers who bring nothing relevant to the program, instead needing to have everything given to them from the time they walk through the door.

As **recipients**, youth are treated like customers who simply walk through the door, consume what they choose, and walk away with their needs met.

When they're treated like **informants**, youth tell adults what they want to hear and leave adults satisfied because they believe they know what youth want, think, or know.

6

The other popular way youth are treated in traditional programs is as **promoters**. When they're promoters, youth are treated like advertisers and promoters who share the ideas of their programs for adults.

Traditional youth programming focused on these roles:

Youth as Receptacles
Treats the experiences, ideas, and knowledge of young people as unimportant or meaningless by allowing adults to "dump" their knowledge on youth without their input.

Youth as Recipients
The notion that children and youth are incapable of making or taking informed, practical, and powerful choices and action that affects themselves and others.

Youth as Informants
Children and youth know things about children and youth, and that much cannot be disputed. Focus groups, advisory boards, interviews… all information sources, all for different reasons.

Youth as Promoters
"Who better to sell stuff to youth than youth themselves?" That quickly explains why mall stores can pay so little to workers – they want youth to work there, and presumably youth can live on less because of their reliance on their parents.

The Change

With the development of new technology, new learning experiences, and different avenues for participation throughout our communities, young people have assumed, been assigned, and have co-created new roles. Programs position participants in many ways, including youth as drivers, facilitators, organizers, and specialists.

As **drivers**, youth are acknowledged for their capacities to motivate and sustain the processes and outcomes they're targeted with.

When they're involved as **facilitators**, young people teach, lead, operate, and guide activities by working in equitable ways with adults. Organizing programming comes as second nature to some youth, as they align activities with goals, develop activities and processes for participants, and position the programs in strategic ways to meet the needs of the organization.

Finally, as **specialists** youth have opportunities to develop, implement, and share the expertise, knowledge, and wisdom they've established, and to critically examine what is done to them.

Following are some examples of roles youth can have in Youth-Driven Programming.

Youth as Drivers
Young people are positioned in formal and informal ways to allow them to move adults and other young people to action. They may be called leaders, evaluators, or advocates, or treated in ways that are engaged and powerful.

Youth as Facilitators
Knowledge comes from study, experience, and reflection. Engaging young people as teachers helps reinforce their commitment to learning and the subject they are teaching; it also engages both young and older learners in exciting ways.

Youth as Organizers
Community organizing happens when leaders bring together everyone in a community in a role that fosters social change. Youth community organizers focus on issues that affect themselves and their communities; they rally their peers, families, and community members for action.

Youth as Specialists

Envisioning roles for youth to teach youth is relatively easy; seeing new roles for youth to teach adults is more challenging. Youth specialists bring expert knowledge about particular subjects to programs and organizations, enriching everyone's ability to be more effective.

Youth-Driven Programs can also engage youth as… Advisors, designers, teachers, grant-makers, planners, lobbyists, trainers, philanthropists, politicians, recruiters, social entrepreneurs, paid staff, mentors, decision makers, activity leaders, policy makers, and more.

Every position is different, offering a variety of perspectives and actions for youth to share their perspectives and take action.

The Differences

The differences in these approaches are vital for understanding the capacity of Youth-Driven Programming to change the lives of individual youth, as well as the organizations and larger communities they belong to.

Youth-Driven Programming is a logical starting point for any organization that wants to serve young people more effectively. It is also a powerful avenue for actually changing the lives of young people.

It can help communities truly sustain young peoples' engagement throughout society. That means acknowledging what young people already know, expanding their exposure to, knowledge of, and opportunities to generate new thinking.

All of the models above can help communities weave an intricate blanket of engagement that swirls within people for all their lives. Youth-driven programs can't have a higher purpose.

Engaging young people through Youth-Driven Programming isn't dependent on formal positions though. Creating youth-driven opportunities throughout organizations and programs allows young people to experience powerful, meaningful transforming in real time.

No matter what avenue your organization takes, it's always important to reinforce that authority through substantial acknowledgment in front of young people and their peers.

Section 3.

Readiness Survey

Read each sentence below then check the box in the same line.

		Agree	Not Sure	Disagree
1.	I think Youth-Driven Programming is important to my organization's future.	☐	☐	☐
2.	I want Youth-Driven Programming throughout our organization.	☐	☐	☐
3.	I need young people and adults to show interest in Youth-Driven Programming before I start.	☐	☐	☐
4.	I am capable of facilitating Youth-Driven Programming right now.	☐	☐	☐
5.	I think Youth-Driven Programming can succeed in my organization.	☐	☐	☐
6.	I know one other adult who cares about Youth-Driven Programming.	☐	☐	☐

7.	I believe young people have a right to be engaged throughout our organization.	☐	☐	☐
8.	I believe young people are capable of things I have not seen.	☐	☐	☐
9.	I know there are young people who count on me.	☐	☐	☐
10.	I know adults who care about young people.	☐	☐	☐
11.	I have valuable insight that is important to Youth-Driven Programming.	☐	☐	☐
12.	I can trust young people in my organization to take Youth-Driven Programming.	☐	☐	☐
13.	I think Youth-Driven Programming has a larger role throughout our community.	☐	☐	☐
14.	I understand how community Youth-Driven Programming works.	☐	☐	☐

15. I believe young people can positively change our community. ☐ ☐ ☐

18. I know adults want to change the roles of young people in our organization. ☐ ☐ ☐

19. I believe young people are important to society. ☐ ☐ ☐

20. I will apply anything I learned from this guide immediately. ☐ ☐ ☐

Section 4.

Check Your Perspective

The ways we see people determine how we treat them. This is especially true between youth and adults. Adult perspectives of youth are obvious in their attitudes about youth, and they are revealed through program planning, activity facilitation, and evaluations.

In public health, education, community development, government, and the environment, Youth-Driven Programming can move from peripheral action to the center of actions intended for young people. However, it's the type of perspectives adults have of children and youth that determines whether Youth-Driven Programming happens.

Adult perspectives also determine the quality, efficacy, and sustainability of Youth-Driven Programming. Culture, education, religion, governmental laws, and economics reinforce these perspectives.

PERSPECTIVES OF YOUNG PEOPLE

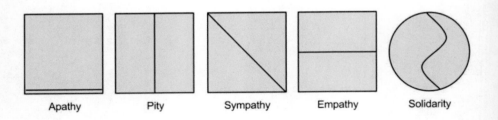

| Apathy | Pity | Sympathy | Empathy | Solidarity |

Following are explanations of each perspective. Each shares what it means, what it does and how it affects Youth-Driven Programming.

Apathy

The first perspective adults have of young people is apathy. Apathy happens when adults consciously or unconsciously choose to be indifferent toward young people. Adults choose not to see children and youth. Mutually enacted upon by both youth and adults.

Pity

After apathy is a completely top-down perspective by adults towards young people called **pity**. Viewing young people with pity actively places adults in a position of complete superiority over children and youth. It positions young people as being completely incapable of providing anything for themselves. By positioning adults in absolute authority, pity extinguishes young peoples' self-esteem and incapacitates their developing senses of agency and purpose. When adults see young people with people, they dehumanize children and youth.

Sympathy

Perceiving youth with **sympathy** can be alluring to adults. It allows adults to give to children and youth what they apparently cannot acquire for themselves, and to do that from a position of compassion. This includes material, teaching, emotional support, or otherwise. However, sympathy disengages young people from actively cultivating what they need for themselves. It singularly positions adults to give to children and youth without acknowledging they are receiving anything from them in return.

Empathy

Perceptions of young people take a completely positive turn when **empathy** is the lens we look through. Reciprocity is the key to establishing empathy with young people. Empathy allows adults to see young people in a more equitable way by identifying that they are receiving something as well as giving it. Adults acknowledge young people as partners, and vice versa. Each becomes invested in the others' perception.

Solidarity

The last perception of **solidarity** is reflected in completely honest, completely equitable relationships between young people and adults. This perception fully recognizes the benefits and challenges in relationships between adults and young people, and operates from a place of possibilities rather than problems. It may be the most challenging perception to maintain because of its completely alien existence throughout our society.

Summary

There are many important things to know about adult perceptions of young people. One is that adults do not maintain one perception of all children and youth all the time. While there are dominant perceptions, there are also exceptions. That is why some young people experience Youth-Driven Programming and others do not, even within the same organization or program. Another thing to know is that these perceptions are not about good or bad—they simply are. Adults do not operate in complete empathy towards young people all the time; likewise, young people should not try to care for every adult they ever meet.

Using these perceptions of young people as a starting point, the challenge for adults in Youth-Driven Programming becomes whether they can consciously, critically, and creatively reflect on their attitudes, behaviors, and ultimately, their perceptions. Next are ways to determine your goals for Youth-Driven Programming, which will show how that reflection can happen.

Section 5.

Locations for Youth-Driven Programming

Although you make work in one organization doing one job, there are countless locations for Youth-Driven Programming to happen throughout your work. These locations include the places Youth-Driven Programming happens, and the ways it happens.

Following is a map of some places for Youth-Driven Programming.

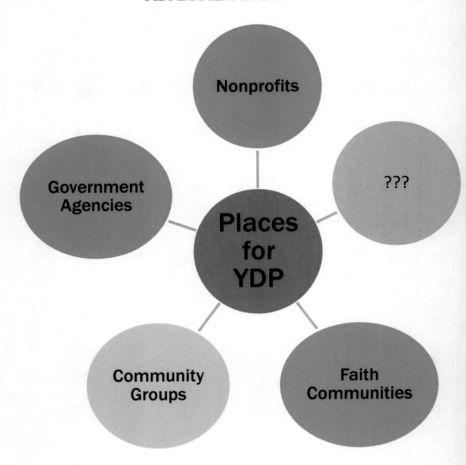

Once you've considered the places Youth-Driven Programming can happen, you should consider the ways it happens.

The following list has 30 different ways youth can drive programming in each of these places. None of these activities is inherently better than others, and none of them guarantee outcomes. However, all of them can be powerful and can transform organizations and communities, as well as the youth who are engaged in them.

30 Ways Youth-Driven Programming Happens in Communities

1. Community Evaluations. When youth evaluate themselves, their homes, their neighborhoods, the activities, physical environment, or other parts of the community, they're participating in Youth-Driven Programming. It can be easy to incorporate listening to Youth-Driven Programming this way- but it doesn't mean anything unless action comes from it.

2. Nonprofit and Government Boardrooms. Youth can present ideas, share concerns, and sit through board and committee meetings just like adults. When nonprofit and government boards involve youth as representatives of their peers, they are listening to youth. However, Youth-Driven Programming means giving youth full-voting positions in decision-making.

3. Community Planning. Youth-Driven Programming in community planning includes creating neighborhood culture, planning community activities and programs, promoting neighborhood improvement, and designing the physical environment. Youth-Driven Programming happens throughout these processes and procedures with intention and purpose.

4. Nonprofit Youth Activities. Adults drive almost all traditional youth programs. When youth talk to each other and adults, they're trying to drive programs. Youths' behavior, attitudes, and actions are also attempts to drive programs. Youth-Driven Programming positions these attempts strategically, and gives youth purpose, power, and possibilities.

5. Streets. When a youth graffitis on the wall "Smithtown sux!", they're sharing trying to drive society. So are youth who fight, form cliques, and play pickup basketball. Youth informally drive neighborhoods all the time, with or without adult supervision and/or approval.

6. Neighborhood Research. Youth who research their communities examine life in all forms, including peoples' behavior, neighborhood funding, laws and policies, and more for efficacy and purpose. Both sharing and collecting data, youth researchers can identify gaps and secure data in ways that many adult researchers cannot.

7. School Protests. Student-led school advocacy can include school protests. When adults don't engage student voice in meaningful ways throughout the school environment, students may feel compelled to make their voices heard by adults. This is one way how that happens.

8. Policy-Making. More than one youth activism group has the motto, "Nothing about me without me," and they are frequently talking about community policy-making. Often the target of formal decisions in nonprofits and governments, youth are rarely engaged in the processes that affect them most.

9. Government Reform. Where adults stand on either side of a city council meeting and poke sticks at each other in the name of improving government, they frequently lose sight of youth. They do this because they haven't engaged youth as partners in government reform. Youth-Driven Programming can lead governments to engage youth in sharing what they think about government and democracy, and they can improve. Youth-Driven Programming engages youth partners through substantive roles in government reform activities.

10. Afterschool. Youth-Driven Programming can drive all afterschool activities, both educational and recreational, in school and otherwise. Youth can plan, evaluate, facilitate, research, advocate, and more for the activities designed to serve them.

11. Youth Clubs. Clubs and other extracurricular activities give the appearance of being an appropriate outlet for Youth-Driven Programming. Club activities must be integrated into daily life and supported throughout the day to be an effective avenue for Youth-Driven Programming.

12. Teaching. Youth-Driven Programming in teaching means giving youth opportunities to teach other youth, adults, and younger people. This can happen through curriculum planning and delivery.

13. Calendar Planning. Looking over the scope of activities gives youth insight into how programs operate. Youth-Driven Programming can inform and drive calendar planning for the whole community.

14. Sports. Sports for youth are popular, and adults' responses to youth have varied. Youth-Driven Programming can allow sports to can share a lot, including essential play information and more.

15. Staff Hiring. Hiring adults to work with youth throughout the community is generally done by adults. However, Youth-Driven Programming in staff hiring, administrator hiring, and the hiring of other adults can help foster environments that are more responsive, safe, and supportive for youth *and* adults.

16. Political Rallies. Youth-Driven Programming in political rallies has to extend beyond simply using youth to decorate adult causes. Engaging youth as partners in planning, facilitating, and participating throughout political rallies is authentic.

17. Rules and Guidelines. When youth help make program guidelines, organizational policies, and government regulations, Youth-Driven Programming is effectively infused in behavior management. Youth courts are another approach, as is having youth engaged in deciding remediation and conflict resolution.

18. Program Planning. Program planning can be made richer and more effective through Youth-Driven Programming. By participating as partners, youth can help decide topic areas, curricular approaches, teaching methods, and other essential parts of the process. Youth-Driven Programming can be most effective in equal partnerships through regular program committees, as well as individual adult leader planning.

19. Government Offices. Towns, cities, counties, states, and regional governments can use Youth-Driven Programming throughout their processes. Grant planning, delivery, and evaluation; policy creation

and evaluation; community improvement planning; building assessment; and many more locations throughout government administration are some locations for Youth-Driven Programming.

20. Organization Technology. Youth-Driven Programming in education technology begins with engaging youth in teaching other youth and adults about technology. Youth can also maintain and develop technology infrastructure in communities, and design tech policies for programs, organizations, and other levels.

21. Adult Training. When youth teach adults about youth culture, student rights, learning styles, and other topics important to them in schools, Youth-Driven Programming is being meaningfully infused in teacher training.

22. Leaders' Offices. Youth-Driven Programming in organizational and community leaders' offices has an important role in decision-making on the personal level and affecting all youth and the larger community. In addition to advocating for themselves, youth can work with leaders to affect community improvement through Youth Action Councils and other formal and informal mechanisms.

23. Grant Evaluations. Evaluating the efficacy of the grant-making designed to serve them positions Youth-Driven Programming to impact communities beyond the youth. Adults can gain important skills and perspectives, as well as energy for implementation, while youth gain important understanding about the purpose of funding for their communities.

24. Organization or Community Budgeting. Engaging youth as partners in complex organizational and government budgeting gives Youth-Driven Programming a purposeful outlet to affect the social system.

25. Playgrounds. When Youth-Driven Programming functions on playgrounds, playing and conflicts have purpose that can be captured for learning and growth. Observing, but not facilitating, playground interactions allows adults to help youth navigate where and how to use their voice appropriately in interpersonal relationships, as well as community-wide applications.

26.   Neighborhood Culture. The attitudes, policies, and structures of a community may change when Youth-Driven Programming drives activities. Culture includes the spoken and unspoken norms in a neighborhood, as well as the beliefs, ideas, actions, and outcomes of youth and adults.

27.   Eating and Food. Youth-Driven Programming in eating and food extends far beyond youth complaints about food quality. Youth are rallying communities to grow locally, provide healthy consumer options, improve menu selection and pricing, and eliminate competitive foods from schools, and more.

28.   Community Design. Youth-Driven Programming can be engaged throughout community design processes and in all age levels. From design to redesign to improvement to reconstruction, Youth-Driven Programming can inform, co-design, and implement community planning in all areas.

29.   In the News. Its increasingly popular to quote youth in education articles. Engaging Youth-Driven Programming in the news includes that, as well as youth-created articles for mainstream websites and newspapers, youth-led video, youth-driven twitter feeds, and other news distribution channels.

30.   Committees. Youth-Driven Programming in decision-making committees can happen within organizations and throughout governments. Youth can participate as full partners in policy-making, grant distribution, curriculum selection, adult hiring and firing, and more.

Section 6.

What Are Your Goals?!?

Before you go further, name your goals for Youth-Driven Programming. Below are four main reasons why people want young people to drive decision-making.

Goals of Youth-Driven Programming

I want to engage youth.

My org wants youth to connect with us and the issue(s) we address.

We want youth to participate in their community.

Attendance should ensure youth are safe and supported.

Youth-Driven Programming can have many goals. However, there are several ways we can measure them. The following four goals for Youth-

24

Driven Programming are not about seeing what is better than or worse than the other—each one has a time and place. What they provide is a glimpse into the actual outcomes of Youth-Driven Programming and give us a simple way to assess where a program is at, and where it can go!

Goal 1: Attendance
Attendance is the act of arriving to a thing outside oneself. Attendance makes sure youth are safe and supported in a place.

Goal 2: Participation
Participation is the self-driven investment of personal energy in a thing. When youth participate in activities, they arrive and belong on their own.

Goal 3: Connection
Connection is an attachment of meaning, purpose, or belonging. Youth who are connected show attachment to other people, activities or issues that matter to them.

Goal 4: Engagement
Engagement is the sustained connection felt with a thing outside oneself. When youth are engaged, they feel a long-term, meaningful and substantive belonging and purpose in the activities they are driving.

Some organizations make the mistake of declaring their goal is one thing, but take actions that lead to a different goal. By examining your intentions, you can identify what you true goal is. If your goal is engagement, youth-driven programming may be the best path to get there!

The following section shows how to do just that.

Section 7.

Planning Youth-Driven Programming

There are things that every adult can do to promote successful Youth-Driven Programming. My experience working with young people has shown me that these things generally fall in sequence. When I follow them I am successful in engaging youth in leading programs met for them.

10 STEPS TO PLAN YOUTH-DRIVEN PROGRAMMING

Following these steps could allow you experience the benefits of youth-driven programming.

Before you do anything...

Step 1: Youth Identify the Goals
- ✓ Why do youth want to use YDP?
- ✓ What does YDP look like to youth?
- ✓ Can YDP make a difference in your organization or community?
- ✓ What are youth going to do next?

Step 2: Youth to Advocate Action
- ✓ Reach from the grassroots and to the treetops.
- ✓ Provide support to take youth places and do things.
- ✓ Build a network of youth advocates focusing on different issues, together.
- ✓ Support youth in learning about broad issues without adult-driven opinions.

Step 3: Youth Secure Support

✓ Take youth directly to decision-makers to influence their process.
✓ Ensure that your organization or community leaders, members, and others are on board with YDP.
✓ Work with youth as a partner to ensure their message is communicated successfully.

Step 4: Youth Plan Programming

✓ Identify what the process and activities are to reach the goals of YDP.

During Action...

Step 5: Prepare Participants

✓ Train youth and adults who are directly and indirectly involved.
✓ Offer supplies and materials to support action.
✓ If asked, provide strategic considerations for participants to think about.

Step 6: Modify Procedures

✓ Make sure the highest authorities in your program, agency or community have signed off on YDP.
✓ Identify activities, train processes, and share new ways of doing things to reflect YDP values.
✓ Work with youth to create a checklist of processes and procedures that reflect YDP, and help youth hold adults accountable to changing those.

Step 7: Reform Policies

✓ Identify policies that need to change to reflect YDP.
✓ Develop organizational and community guidelines, rules, and laws to ensure fidelity to YDP.
✓ Create an assessment to make sure change is happening.

Step 8: Develop Structures
✓ Create a youth-driven group to make sure there are high amounts of accountability for YDP.
✓ Develop lasting organizational and community infrastructure that ensures sustained YDP.
✓ Build a long-term budget that takes into account changed actions and outcomes from YDP.

Step 9: Transform Culture
✓ Offer ongoing training and materials to support increased investment in YDP.
✓ Intention and time will allow for organizational and community cultures to transform and become more reflective of YDP.
✓ Work with youth to create an assessment that holds adults and organizations accountable for YDP.

Step 10: Critically Challenge
✓ Train youth and adults about critical perspectives.
✓ Give room for youth and adults to critically reflect, expose, examine, and determine next steps for action and change.
✓ Create a forum for specific and healthy exchanges of critical opinions between youth and adults, youth and youth, and the community at large.

DOS AND DON'TS
FOR PLANNING YOUTH-DRIVEN PROGRAMMING

To plan Youth-Driven Programming, **DO**…
- ✓ Bring groups of youth together to adult events.
- ✓ Acknowledge youth the same as you do adult participants.
- ✓ Seek nontraditional youth leaders to share their voices.
- ✓ Present the context to adults and youth for why youth are participating.
- ✓ Plan on reporting the outcomes of the event to youth participants as well as adults.
- ✓ Make sure youth are present anytime you discuss Youth-Driven Programming.
- ✓ Learn to make room for youth to share their wisdom, ideas, knowledge, and experiences in organizations or communities.
- ✓ Explore different ways to engage youth as partners in community change.
- ✓ Ensure when young people share relevant personal information that adults share the same amount of info.
- ✓ Make every effort to ensure youth involvement is a sustained activity, not just a one-time exception.

To plan Youth-Driven Programming, **DON'T**…
- ✗ Assume youth needed special motivation to become involved; treat them like interested parties.
- ✗ Invite one youth speaker to talk at an adult event; bring a group.
- ✗ Only invite adult-pleasing youth to participate in Youth-Drive Programming.
- ✗ Seek out one, two, or ten youth as the most popular in their organization or communities to represent youth.
- ✗ Fail to explain to youth how they were selected for an activity.
- ✗ Forget to tell adults and youth the purpose of engaging youth.
- ✗ Don't explain to youth which youth they are supposed to represent.
- ✗ Invite one youth speaker to talk at an adult event; bring a group.

✗ Seek out one, two, or ten youth as the most popular in their organizations or communities to represent youth.

✗ Fail to explain to youth how they were selected for an activity.

✗ Forget to tell adults and youth the purpose of engaging youth.

✗ Don't explain to youth which youth they are supposed to represent.

Section 8.

Preparing participants

Preparing participants for Youth-Driven Programming can happen in a number of ways, including shifting attitudes, training skills, and building confidence. Before any of that, advocates for Youth-Driven Programming should build awareness.

Different Approaches to Youth-Driven Programming

One tool to help to this is the Spectrum of Youth-Driven Programming. It is designed to help adults think about how they interact with youth personally, and in their organizations. Sometimes YDP is confused with traditional youth programs because people do not consider these different ways.

SPECTRUM OF YOUTH-DRIVEN PROGRAMMING

This Spectrum works differently with different people in different places at different times. The most important thing to know is that no single youth or adult stays in one place on the Spectrum at all times. Instead, this is a tool meant to show fluidity and responsiveness. There are times, places, people, and purposes that require anyone who is involved to assume different positions at different times.

Following are descriptions of each place on this spectrum. Keep the previous paragraph in mind as you read each of them.

Assigned and Informed

The first way to prepare participants for Youth-Driven Programming is to assign them to get involved and inform them about what is going to happen. You can do this by providing materials or websites about youth voice, youth involvement, youth activism, or youth leadership. This relies on youth and adults taking initiative to learn more on their own, and does not acknowledge differences of opinion, perspectives, or ideas.

Informed and Consulted

Preparing participants for Youth-Driven Programming can mean informing them about what's going to happen and consulting them to find out what they think. Their responses may or may not actually inform the activity, since they are not fully equitable. However, they are still youth-driven because youth have shared their opinions and they have informed programming.

Volunteer and Equal

When participants step up and want to get involved and are treated equally, they need to be prepared for action. Training should include preparing for action, gathering more knowledge, reflecting on experiences, or other activities that treat participants in equal ways. This treatment doesn't treat people as individuals and emphasizes equality before genuine needs.

Youth-Led

Preparing participants for youth-led action may include building the capacity of youth and adults to become involved and contribute in meaningful ways. It can include a variety of activities and outcomes, as long as they stay youth-driven without adults. This is what many people associate with Youth-Driven Programming.

Equitable Partnerships

The final role considers the different capacities of children and youth in relationship to those with adults. Seeing that everyone is operating from a different place for different purposes, Youth-Driven Programming employing equitable partnerships may include preparing participants to be engaged in training, research, planning, teaching, evaluating and advocacy, all done in partnerships between youth and adults.

ADAM FLETCHER

DOS AND DON'TS
FOR PREPARING YOUTH-DRIVEN PROGRAMMING

When planning Youth-Driven Programming, adults should consider the following dos and don'ts.

To prepare participants for Youth-Driven Programming, **DON'T**...

x Talk down to youth; just because they're younger doesn't mean they're dumber.
x Single out one youth for their race, socio-economic class, sexual orientation, academic performance, etc.
x Underemphasize the democratic purpose of Youth-Driven Programming.
x Neglect to explain to youth why they're involved in an activity.
x Make youth less than adults; youth should have opportunities with adults in activities.
x Forget to give youth plenty of opportunity to formulate their own opinions before speaking.

To prepare participants for Youth-Driven Programming, **DO**...

✓ Teach youth about the society and cultures they participate in.
✓ Teach youth jargon, theory, issues, and strategies.
✓ Help youth learn about the broad issues in society affecting them.
✓ Encourage and facilitate youth talking with each other before they participate in Youth-Driven Programming.
✓ Invite youth to assert themselves *as they see fit*, including sharing real experiences and saying what works.
✓ Let youth know their participation is crucial to the success of organizations.
✓ Encourage and facilitate active adult interaction with the youth at events.

Section 9.

Facilitating Programs

Facilitating Youth-Driven Programming requires that adults move beyond whole group facilitation and use other methods. Interaction is essential for Youth-Driven Programming. Many program activities can benefit from using strategies that go beyond facilitating large groups by focusing on different configurations of activities. By its nature, Youth-Driven Programming keeps youth and adult participants energized and fully engaged.

A lot of people try to facilitate Youth-Driven Programming for large groups. That is not an impossible thing to do, but its important to remember that paying attention to individual youth is at the heart of Youth-Driven Programming. Here are four different ways you can facilitate YDP beyond large groups:

Subgroups
Count off subgroups, and assign them the task of thinking about large group activities. Try a focus question, and ask the subgroup to present what they learned back to the large group.

Partners
Invite pairs or trios to discuss a focus question together for a short time. Get highlights and write them down during report out.

Go-arounds
Once the highlight info has been shared, help the conversation open up to quieter participants. Invite a short, timed go-round so that everyone has an equal chance for sharing.

Polling

After group discussion has gone on for a while, invite a straw poll through a show of hands, e.g., " on a scale of 1 to 5, how much do you agree with _____?", then discuss the reasons that people voted as they did.

DOS AND DON'TS
FOR FACILITATING YOUTH-DRIVEN
PROGRAMMING

To facilitate Youth-Driven Programming, **DON'T**...

✘ Give the impression that Youth-Driven Programming only happens at your organization.

✘ Isolate youth from adults, either in small groups or overall, without thorough consideration.

✘ Ask youth to address topics they could know nothing about without preparation.

✘ Call on one particular youth to share repeatedly.

✘ Instruct youth to make generalizations about other youth.

✘ Only invite 10 youth to join 1,000 adults at an event; aim for equal numbers.

✘ Limit youth to talk about topics adults think they should instead of other issues.

✘ Put youth in traditional adult positions without the authority, ability, or knowledge adults usually receive.

✘ Neglect to tell all people present—adults and youth—the purpose of Youth-Driven Programming and their involvement.

✘ Undermine Youth-Driven Programming by letting adults and youth think that youth are being tokenized.

✘ Treat Youth-Driven Programming as unique, infallible, or otherwise put youth on a pedestal.

To facilitate Youth-Driven Programming, **DO**...

✓ Tell and engage youth in multiple roles beyond being informants for adults.

✓ See and treat Youth-Driven Programming as integral to organizations and communities.

✓ Share with youth and adults that youth only represent themselves and their own experiences.

✓ Acknowledge youth the same way adults are acknowledged for attending.

✓ Simply listen to the words and ways youth talk about issues, and ask for clarification when needed.

✓ Allow youth to drive programs in informal ways (speaking, writing, art, Internet) and not formal ways (board and staff positions, policies, program leadership).

✓ Give youth the explicit right and opportunities to raise issues and to fully participate in activities.

✓ Treat engaging youth as a culture to foster, not a checkbox to complete.

✓ Allow youth to talk on an organization's social media sites and at in-person activities.

✓ See and treat youth as full partners throughout society.

✓ Engage youth in issues at the local building level, not in district, state, or federal activities.

Section 10.

Founding Programs

In order to create real social change, it is vital for all Youth-Driven Programming to build and maintain their operations. Research has shown founding programs intentionally is crucial for youth themselves, as well as the organizations and communities where they're engaged.

Following are eight elements to establish a foundation for Youth-Driven Programming. which in turn can help the long-term sustainability of Youth-Driven Programming. Decide which are important for you and target them. As you complete one, add another until all have been addressed.

8 Elements in the Foundation of Youth-Driven Programming

1. Vision
Have a clear-cut vision for Youth-Driven Programming is basic and essential. In order to develop a meaningful vision, make sure it is owned by *YOU*, shared by leaders and driven by youth themselves. They should create it, act as caretakers and advocates for it, hold it and critique it.

2. Results Orientation
Estimate and demonstrate how Youth-Driven Programming will affect participants, organizations, and communities.

3. Strategic Funding Orientation
Show that Youth-Driven Programs are able to maintain funding in short- and long-term. Do this by operating on nimble budgets, fostering sustainable funding relationships, and building ownership for the vision among as many youth and adults as possible.

4. Adaptability to Changing Conditions

As communities, politics, organizational leadership, and youth themselves change, show that Youth-Driven Programs are capable of changing with them. Ensure that community leaders, parents, educators, politicians, foundations, nonprofit volunteers and others are all equally and meaningfully invested in Youth-Driven Programming.

5. Broad Base of Community Support

Build and maintain support for Youth-Driven Programming beyond individual adults and youth by engaging parents, business owners, community leaders, faith leaders, and others.

6. Key Champions

Maintain a group of youth and adults who believe, support, and rally others to support Youth-Driven Programming.

7. Strong Internal Systems

Develop strong training, governance, accounting, information, and participant recruitment and retention systems to ensure the success of Youth-Driven Programming.

8. Sustainability Plan

Sustainability plans help current and future Youth-Driven Program advocates and facilitators maintain fidelity and clarify action, goals, and outcomes.

DOS AND DON'TS
FOR SUSTAINING YOUTH-DRIVEN PROGRAMMING

To sustain Youth-Driven Programming, **DON'T**…

✗ Treat youth favorably for driving programming in an a way you approve of.

✗ Punish youth when Youth-Driven Programming doesn't meet adult expectations.

✗ Invite youth to share their knowledge, ideas, opinions, and more, and then not use what they say.

✗ Neglect to recognize youth learning through Youth-Driven Programming with class credit.

✗ Deny the absence of Youth-Driven Programming in local organizations if adults or youth raise the issue.

✗ Acknowledge the validity of Youth-Driven Programming that adults might disagree with.

✗ Ask youth to participate in Youth-Driven Programming that never affects the communities they're from.

✗ Interpret and reinterpret Youth-Driven Programming into activities, language, acronyms, purposes, and outcomes that adults use.

To sustain Youth-Driven Programming, **DO**...

✓ Encourage mutual accountability between youth and adults.

✓ Engage youth in as many topics as possible, and don't ignore it regarding others.

✓ Create ongoing opportunities to listen to youth and engage youth as partners.

✓ Get past one-time activities by encouraging regular organizational-level and classroom-level youth activities.

✓ Encourage different youth to participate across activities.

✓ Create "safe spaces" where youth can stay connected in the long-term after events.

✓ Engage adults and youth as full partners in taking action.

✓ Share freechild.org as a resource, including examples, tools, links, and more.

Section 11.

Scaffolding for Youth-Driven Programming*

The support device called scaffolding which is used for building and maintaining buildings has two parts, the scaffolds and the supports. This section identifies what the scaffolds and supports are for Youth-Driven Programming.

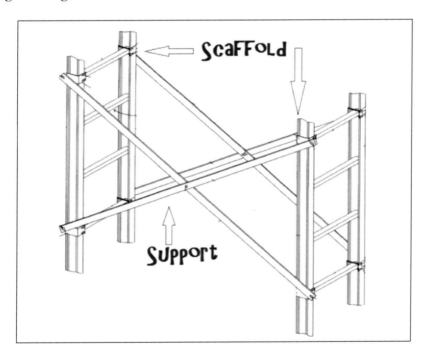

After you've ensured that you have a firm foundation to build upon, you need to scaffold Youth-Driven Programming in order to ensure its effective, substantive, and sustainable. This scaffolding will do more to ensure success than any other thing you can do.

The following questions were based on the work of an UK researcher named Michael Fielding. They are intended to walk you through some of the basic components for successful programs.

Support: Involvement

✓ Who is involved in Youth-Driven Programming, and how are they involved?
   ★ Which youth are allowed to be involved in driving programming?
   ★ Who are youth allowed to drive programs for?
   ★ What are youth allowed to create programming focused on?
   ★ What language, behaviour, and activities are encouraged and/or allowed

Scaffold: Attitudes

✓ How do the young people and adults involved regard each other?
✓ To what degree are the principle of equal value and the dispositions of care felt reciprocally and demonstrated through the reality of daily encounter?
✓ Are the skills of Youth-Driven Programming encouraged and supported through training or other appropriate means?
✓ Are these skills understood, developed and practiced within the context of other democratic values and dispositions?
✓ Are these skills themselves changed or informed by those values and dispositions?

Scaffold: Systems

✓ How often does dialogue and engagement between youth and adults currently

✓ Who feels responsible for Youth-Driven Programming?
✓ What happens if aspirations and good intentions are not realized?
✓ How do the systems highlighting the value and necessity of Youth-Driven Programming mesh with other activities, especially those involving adults?
✓ What action is taken for Youth-Driven Programming?

Scaffold: Culture

✓ Do cultural norms and values proclaim the importance of Youth-Driven Programming within the context of communities as a shared responsibility and shared achievement?
✓ Do the practices, traditions and routine daily encounters demonstrate values supportive of Youth-Driven Programming?

Support: The Future

✓ Do we need new structures for Youth-Driven Programming?
✓ Do we need new ways of relating to each other as youth and/or adults?

Section 12.

Assessing Youth-Driven Programming

Will Rogers once wrote, "Even if you're on the right track you can still get run over if you don't move." These rubrics are to help you assess the strongest applications of Youth-Driven Programming.

✓ Fast Track The goal is engaging all youth and sustaining the impacts.
✓ On Track Everything's intact but not really effective or sustainable.
✓ Sidetracked Well-intended action is poorly thought-through and implemented.

Rubric One: Youth-Driven Learning

Goal	Fast Track	On Track	Sidetracked
Stronger Learning Connections	Youth & adults collaborate to design, implement, evaluate learning activities.	Adults facilitate youth-informed learning activities.	Youth graded on their engagement in learning without any input into teaching.
Greater Youth Authority	Activities co-taught by youth with adults as mentors.	Solely youth-led activities throughout the programming.	Adult self-designs programming and claim it is Youth-Driven Programming.
Learning Improvement Efforts	Program is dedicated to engaging youth throughout learning improvement efforts.	Youth encouraged to use out-of-school time to engage themselves and others to improve learning.	Youth taught about effects of learning improvement without knowing how they can assist or challenge it.

Rubric Two: Youth-Driven Community Groups

Goal	Fast Track	On Track	Sidetracked
Secure Public Commitment	Organization makes its youth-drivenness apparent in all activities, policies, and publicity.	Dedicated, sustainable, focused youth positions created.	One youth is a member of a board of directors or on a committee.
Increase Staff Responsibility	Youth self-identify issues and resources they need to create change.	Youth are engaged as regular staff or volunteers.	Staff claim to support Youth-Driven Programming while none actually engages youth.
Sustain Long-Term Support	Adult support for youth is made explicit through resource sharing, including fiscal, material, etc.	Staff show full commitment through ongoing training, support, activities, and reflection.	Resources are not allocated to support Youth-Driven Programming in the organization or programs.

Rubric Three: Youth-Driven After School Programs

Goal	Fast Track	On Track	Sidetracked
Increase Program Commitment	Diverse youth initiate, plan, direct, implement, reflect, and evaluate with coaching from adults.	Youth guide some activities with adult mentorship.	Adults lead all activities without regard for youth input or feedback.
Secure Youth Support	Adults provide guidance: coaching, training, resource-sharing, and networking to young people.	Organization follows through with small group of young people.	Adults occasionally seek support of youth when convenient.
Provide Staff Development	Adult staff provided with initial and ongoing training opportunities that grow their commitment and ability.	Adult staff assigned to attend initial training not directly related to Youth-Driven Programming.	Position filled by unsuspecting volunteer operating without training or materials.

Rubric Four: Youth-Driven Philanthropy

Goal	Fast Track	On Track	Sidetracked
Deepen Youth Engagement	Foundation commits to Youth-Driven Programming throughout policy, practice, leadership, and evaluation.	Philanthropy activities heavily support Youth-Driven Programming through funding practices.	Youth-Driven Programming is among unstated funding interests.
Prioritize Funding	Youth involved in determining all priorities, grantees, monitoring, and reflection.	Youth-led funding activities support youth programs.	Youth-Driven Programming is critiqued among applicants and grantees without offering guidance or support.
Transform Giving Strategy	All staff trained in Youth-Driven Programming and programs are underway throughout organization.	Adult staff trained and youth focus groups inform philanthropy.	Carefully selected young people participate in minimal funding activities.

Rubric Five: Youth-Driven Governance

Goal	Fast Track	On Track	Sidetracked
Secure Long-Term Governance Commitment to Youth-Driven Programming	Policies are changed to create permanent positions for young people to propose, influence, and advocate.	Community-wide Youth-Driven Programming devised and implemented with long-range funding.	Community activities and organization committees with no youth, or a citywide youth summit no adults allowed.
Dedicate Personnel to Youth-Driven Programming	Young people are engaged through regular (paid), volunteer, elected, and other opportunities.	Trained staff develop and coordinate Youth-Driven Programming with active volunteer youth advisors.	"Youth councils" and Children's Cabinets made of concerned adults without youth themselves.
Secure Broad Support for Youth-Driven Programming	Activities designed by youth/adult partners to promote Youth-Driven Programming throughout government.	Adults engage youth in advisory committees without actually affecting youth directly.	Youth-Driven Programming training for government workers without youth participants or trainers.

Rubric Six: Youth-Driven Organizational Transformation

Goal	Fast Track	On Track	Sidetracked
Change the Attitude	All members express clear commitment to Youth-Driven Programming.	Leaders express clear commitment to Youth-Driven Programming.	Youth are only people to express clear commitment to Youth-Driven Programming.
Reform Policy	All policies are reformed to include Youth-Driven Programming.	Policies affecting youth reformed to include Youth-Driven Programming.	Other activity is required to participate in Youth-Driven Programming activities.
Transform Culture	Youth-Driven Programming is acknowledged strategy for the organization to promote democracy in their community-building.	Youth-Driven Programming is seen as only strategy for democracy building.	Youth-Driven Programming seen as novel/tokenistic tool for making young people happy or keep them "out of trouble."

Section 13.

Glossary

This is a short glossary of Youth-Driven Programming-related words; learn more at http://goo.gl/qUQzU

Adult Ally
A proactive non-youth who works with or for young people through a non-threatening, anti-discriminatory relationship with them.

Attendance
The act of arriving to a thing outside oneself.

Connection
An attachment of meaning, purpose, or belonging.

Engagement
The sustained connection felt with a thing outside oneself.

Equality
When two people are treated as 50/50 equals to achieve a goal.

Equity
When two people are treated according to their needs, wants, and abilities to achieve a goal.

Participation
The self-driven investment of personal energy in a thing.

Reflection

The deliberate examination, exploration, or recollection of personal and/or collective actions, often to establish connections between action and intentions.

Tokenism

Making someone represent all others of a particular type.

Youth

Anyone under the age of majority in a community or organization, which is generally either 25, 21, or 18.

Youth/Adult Partnership

Intentional relationships between young people and adults that build and sustain engagement between generations.

Youth Driven Programming

Any effort led by people under 18, including conceiving, researching, planning, enacting, teaching, evaluating, reflecting, deconstructing, and re-envisioning a program.

Youth Voice

The active, distinct, and concentrated ways young people represent themselves throughout society.

Section 14.
Youth-Driven Programming Resources

Examples
- Pennsylvania. Strengthening Youth Driven Programming in Afterschool: DARE's Youth Driven Programming Initiative— http://goo.gl/dQf4v
- New Mexico. KUNM Youth Radio— http://goo.gl/ic2ps
- Connecticut. Perrin Family Foundation— http://goo.gl/az4Mo
- North Carolina. Youth-Empowered Solutions— http://goo.gl/oyFqh
- Missouri. "Program works to control tobacco"— http://goo.gl/Mgx0Z
- Washington. Wilderness Inner-City Leadership Development— http://goo.gl/xBRF2

Tools
- "Youth-Driven Space: Formative Index"— http://goo.gl/WNgwT
- "Youth-Driven Program Fact Sheet"— http://goo.gl/pdPde
- *Youth Development & Youth Leadership*—http://goo.gl/R7YNH
- *Washington Youth Voice Handbook*— http://freechild.org/WYVH.htm
- "A Comparison Between Youth-Driven and Adult-Driven Programs: Balancing Inputs from Youth and Adults"— http://goo.gl/8Xhdx

ADAM FLETCHER

About the Author

Adam Fletcher

Adam is a 20-year veteran in the fields of youth development and education. Today, he is an writer and motivational speaker, and the president of CommonAction Consulting. He is the founding director of The Freechild Project and SoundOut, and has authored more than 100 articles and 50 publications related to youth. Adam works with 10,000 children, youth, and adults annually to promote engagement throughout communities.

Learn how to bring Adam to your organization or community by visiting adamfletcher.net

Other Books by Adam Fletcher

The Practice of Youth Engagement, 2014;
School Boards of the Future: Students as Policy-Makers, 2014;
The Guide to Student Voice, 2014;
Ending Discrimination Against Young People, 2013;
SoundOut Student Voice Curriculum, 2013;

The Freechild Project

Transforming the Roles of Young People throughout Society

Since 2001.

freechild.org

Made in the USA
Middletown, DE
20 March 2023